Tiffany White

HEAL GIRL!

You Have the Right to Let Go

Copyright © 2023 by Tiffany White

All rights reserved. This book or parts thereof may not be reproduced, stored in a retrieval system, or transmitted in any form or by any means–electronic, mechanical, photocopy, recording, scanning, or otherwise–except for brief quotations in critical reviews or articles, without the prior written permission of the publisher.

Cover design by Seven FX Creative

Published in West Palm Beach, Florida by Cassy's Touch Publishing, LLC. Cassy's Touch Publishing, LLC books, journals, etc., may be ordered through bookseller or by contacting: www.cassystouch.com

The publisher is not responsible for websites (or their content) that are not owned by the publisher.

Scripture taken from Christian Standard Bible® (CSB). Copyright © 2017 by Holman Bible Publishers. Used by permission. Christian Standard Bible® and CSB® are federally registered trademarks of Holman Bible Publishers.

Visit the author's website at www.simplytiffany.net

ISBN: 979-8-9892358-0-3 (hardcover)
ISBN: 979-8-9892358-1-0 (ebook)
Library of Congress Control Number: 2023921088

Printed in the United States of America

Contents

INTRODUCTION		iv
ONE	Dig Deep	1
TWO	Open Wounds	11
THREE	Healed Vision	20
FOUR	Heal the Unseen	27
FIVE	The Key to a Healed Identity	37
SIX	Your Truth Uncovered	48
SEVEN	Voice Triggers	58
EIGHT	God's Reminder	65
NINE	Familiar Ground	71
TEN	Let Go of the Old Patterns	81
ELEVEN	Control + Alt + Delete	90
TWELVE	Heal Preacher	100
THIRTEEN	I Stopped Breathing	112
FOURTEEN	Let It Go	118
FIFTEEN	FOMO	127
SIXTEEN	Healing Equals Legacy	133
CONCLUSION	The Bottom Line	140
BONUS CHAPTER	War for Your Healing	142
ABOUT THE AUTHOR		161

INTRODUCTION

I don't watch much television because there isn't much on it that grabs my attention. However, during one season of my life, I was hooked on a show that showcased singles going on dates with different people – hoping to find love. One of the young ladies on the show, at that time, was very sensitive because of the unresolved trauma from her past. She was aware of the trauma, but she didn't seem to be fully aware of how her past trauma was affecting her present relationships.

It affected how she carried herself and how she communicated with others – male and female. The perception of what she heard, and saw was perverted because it was tightly knitted with the unresolved trauma from her past.

In one of the first episodes, a guy expressed an interest in her – *only* an interest without commitment. However, she saw his interest as a commitment and later in the *same* episode, she became extremely jealous when the guy was talking (*only talking*) to another woman.

She made a scene and because of the unresolved trauma in her life, she didn't see anything wrong with her behavior.

At that moment, I yelled at my television and said, "You need to heal girl!" I paused. Then, I heard Holy Spirit say, *"That's your next book."*

Seeing how easy it was for me to see her wounds, I thought that this would be an easy book to write. Having the ability to connect, identify, and relate with others who aren't quite healed yet was evidence that *I did my work*; and truth be told, you have to do <u>*a lot*</u> of work to have clarity in an area that you were once blind in – however, the deeper I went in this book, the more I realized the trauma and issues that were unresolved in my life.

The more I wrote, the more I saw thought patterns, belief systems, and behaviors that were not conducive to my development and maturing.

To be quite honest, this book made me very uncomfortable – but discomfort is expected during the healing process. Contrary to our imagination, the healing process is not smooth sailing. It is not pain free. It is not peaceful. When you go through the healing process God's way by remaining committed through the pain, confrontation, and turbulence, you will experience the peace that you've been longing for. You may experience occasional pain from your wounds, but they will no longer hurt from the slightest touch.

You will be able to stand confidently and say, *"I AM HEALED."*

Considering how *HEAL Girl!* was dropped on me, I assumed that this sequel to *HUSH Girl!* would primarily focus on emotional healing. However, as I dived deeper in writing this book, the Lord showed me that the healing that is needed is greater than what's happening emotionally. How a person reacts emotionally is only a response to something that was received physically.

In Acts chapter three, Peter and John healed a lame man who was carried and placed at the entrance of a temple daily. For years, he did what he thought was necessary because of his condition – he begged for money.

Because of this man's condition, he was unable to clearly see what he really needed. He was lame from birth. All he knew was pain. So, his physical condition clouded his emotional being. He was lame but begged for money. Emotionally, he thought that he was doing the right thing. His purpose was to beg, and his physical condition got him there.

His pain told him that living a life as a beggar was the only future for him to survive. He adjusted his life to the pain that stemmed from birth.

To become a beggar means that you have accepted the lack in your life and determined that you, alone, can't fix it – so you make do. You do what it takes to survive. You cover your pain by begging for money. You cover your insecurities by being the center of attention or begging for friends. You cover your low self-esteem by making sure that your appearance is perfect – nothing is out of place. You cover your anxiety by taking medication. You cover your feelings of insufficiency by eating more or eating junk.

Naturally, there isn't anything wrong with some of the lifestyles that I listed above (i.e. your appearance being on point) however, the problem sets in when these behaviors or lifestyles become excessive in an attempt to not deal with the pain that is immobilizing you.

A beggar's behavior is one that is excessive. You always need more. You always need to keep busy. What you receive is never enough; so, you go back to the same place daily to ask for more.

Unresolved pain can make you immobile. It can taint your perspective of what's available to you now, and it can invade your future.

This man accepted his condition because it was all he knew. So, he kept begging – until he met two men who were Jesus followers and were able to see what this lame man really needed.

Peter and John gave this lame man the answer to all of his problems. What's the answer to all of your problems? Do you really believe that Jesus wants to heal you? If you do, then you must commit to stop running from your healing.

Running is very easy to do. It's a natural learned behavior. If you touch the stove while it is hot, then you will naturally pull back quickly in response to the instant pain. So, you naturally learn not to touch a hot stove or to only touch the stove when it's off.

But consider this… although the stove is off and you may never touch a hot stove again, you are still wounded.

You still have to face the pain in order to heal. When the wound becomes ugly or less appealing, you can't pick at it because it will take longer to heal, and you will risk having a bigger scar.

Healing requires stillness. You have to sit in the pain and allow God to heal you.

Are you willing to sit long enough to hear God's voice? Are you still long enough to receive God's touch?

You have to feel the pain before you can experience God's healing.

This book was written to bring healing to the people who unintentionally have become beggars. You accepted the lack in your life because you don't know anything else. You don't know what healing in *your* area of lack would look like for you. Sure, you see other people healed, but because of the depth of the trauma that you have experienced, you're not certain if your healing will look like theirs.

Can I share something with you?

Your healing *will not* look like everyone else's.

Jesus healed hundreds of people and every healing had the same outcome but a different process.

To avoid disappointment in your healing process, don't expect for your process to be the same as anyone else's.

What I've learned is that God has a special way of healing all of us. Submit to His hand, not the idea of His hand.

Healing is yours.

Choose to be committed to God's process and allow Him to heal you in real-time…

It's time for you to HEAL girl!

CHAPTER 1

Dig Deep

It was the end of the school year, and as I was driving to pick up my son, the song *Tell Your Heart to Beat Again* by Danny Gokey came on the radio. It immediately reminded me of a real fragile time in my life where I was completely numb.

A month after my former husband shared that he wanted a divorce, I went away to Orlando, Florida with a few ladies to bond – including my spiritual mom. During our time together, my spiritual mom looked at me and said, *"You need to breathe."* Then, she began to play a song that someone shared with her during a tough time in her life.

It was *Tell Your Heart to Beat Again* – a beautiful song that would awaken anyone who is going through a loss in life. Here are the lyrics to the chorus…

HEAL GIRL

Tell your heart to beat again.
Close your eyes and breathe it in
Let the shadows fall away.
Step into the light of grace
Yesterday's a closing door
You don't live there anymore.
Say goodbye to where you've been.
And tell your heart to beat again.

I listened to the words of the song, but I was completely numb. It was clear to my spiritual mom that I was not present, so she grabbed my foot and began to massage it with hopes that I would snap out of my numb condition, relax, and embrace what I was experiencing so that healing could begin.

She said, *"Embrace this. Sit in it. Breathe and feel. Tell your heart to beat again."*

I just looked at her. I wanted so bad to feel the pain and rejection from my situation, but I couldn't connect.

She massaged my foot for the duration of the song. When it ended, she placed my foot down and I sat there for a moment. Then, I got up and went to my bathroom and just stared at myself in disbelief that I was going through this again. Divorce. I was back at square one.

As traumatizing as divorce can be, it wasn't the source of why I was numb. Numbness doesn't just suddenly appear. In the natural, we experience numbness after sitting or applying pressure to one part of the body for an extended period of time. Unless you change your position, you will feel the sensation of your body gradually losing its feeling. It doesn't happen by surprise.

It wasn't the divorce that led to me not being able to connect with the rest of the world. I didn't allow myself to feel from my first divorce, and as a result, I remained in the same position for years, and being numb became my safe place.

Each heartbeat is necessary because it moves the very thing that carries life to every organ of your body so that you can thrive. Its beats supply oxygen to your body so that you can breathe.

HEAL GIRL

The moment your heart stops beating is the moment that you lose life. Many ignore the pain caused from trauma which results in walking around like a zombie – disconnected, going through the motions, and miserable because your life yields no return. Truth be told, I'm only familiar with it because I was there. I was living but in all that I was doing, I was still unfulfilled.

Being healed goes so much deeper than getting over someone, or something in your life. Being healed is directly connected to your quality of life. It's linked to having fulfillment in life and abundance in your relationships. The quality of your relationships determines the quality of your life.

Comfort and complacency will keep you yoked to an expired season of pain in your life.

If I didn't feel, then I didn't have to deal with what caused me so much pain. I continued to serve others, but I didn't allow myself to "*feel*" or be connected enough to *be served.*

DIG DEEP

It was safe for me to go through the motions and not uncover the wound that needed to be treated. The longer your wounds are untreated, the more susceptible you are to developing an infection that (if not treated), immobilizes you, *and* ultimately takes your life.

Confrontation is necessary – for peace's sake. It unlocks your healing and uncovers the peace that belongs to you. Your peace is wrapped up in your healing.

God wants to serve you. His service to you is healing you. Your pain is not to be ignored. Sometimes it is your pain that launches you into a better season where people are able to experience a better you. The longer you ignore your pain, the longer you ignore your season of better.

I've learned that God gives us the strength to endure the most uncomfortable, painful, and toughest seasons of our lives. Tough seasons expose weaknesses, but that doesn't mean that you are weak.

There is a greater purpose for your weakness.

One of the toughest and strongest men that I know, found himself in a very uncomfortable place. In his weakness, he begged Jesus to take the pain away. But Jesus said…

… *"My grace is sufficient for you, for my power is perfected in weakness."*

Then the Apostle Paul said…

"Therefore, I will most gladly boast all the more about my weaknesses, so that Christ's power may reside in me. So I take pleasure in weaknesses, insults, hardships, persecutions, and in difficulties, for the sake of Christ. For when I am weak, then I am strong." (2 Corinthians 12:9-10)

Pain is a natural response. It is a sign that your body wants to heal. It is a sign that your body doesn't want to stay in the current condition. There is better for you on the other side of pain, but it begins with you having the courage to embrace the pain you feel now so that you can leave where you've been.

DIG DEEP

Seasons can change, and time will move on but if you're trapped in your mind then you won't have the capacity to move forward.

It's time to heal by telling your heart to beat again.

It is my prayer that you will become strengthened to dig deep and open your heart to allow your healing to begin.

HEAL Girl! Because your new season starts now.

You may be numb, tired, and frustrated because you're back to square one. You're back to a place where you hoped you'd never be again. But you're here. The key to getting out of this place is to identify what is keeping you from feeling. What has you numb?

God wants to treat you and sometimes He will send people who will escort you into healing. Will you open your heart for the Him to heal you?

HEAL GIRL

Answer these questions in the space provided below.

_____
_____
_____
_____
_____
_____
_____
_____
_____
_____
_____
_____
_____
_____
_____
_____
_____
_____
_____
_____
_____
_____
_____

DIG DEEP

HEAL GIRL

CHAPTER 2

Open Wounds

It was easy for me to point out the young woman's issues on the television series that I mentioned earlier, because her condition was familiar to me.

As mentioned in *HUSH Girl!: You have the Right to Remain Silent in Life's Questionable Seasons*, I have been married and divorced twice. I know what betrayal feels like and how much of a toll it takes on you mentally and physically.

After finding out about the affair of my son's father and a friend of mine, I struggled with accepting and embracing the weight and level of betrayal that I faced. Mentally, I knew that the right thing to do was to forgive them both, but my heart was broken. It was my deepest desire to forgive both of them completely because I knew that forgiveness would make God smile and, ultimately, it would free me.

Yet, I didn't realize that in order to forgive I had to accept what was happening, and choose to feel the pain that came with it.

My wound was deep and the longer that I ignored it, the more the pain from it manifested in my body. At one point, I was prescribed seven different medications due to the emotional imbalance that I was experiencing.

The medicine helped me function but it continued to cover up the pain that I needed to face. I was walking in denial. Just existing until my issues caught up with me.

You can attempt to run away from your issue, but at some point, your issue will catch up with you. In order to survive, you will need to feel your open wound.

Denial kills. It can kill emotionally, mentally, and naturally.

The first thing that you need to do to experience healing is you must stop and acknowledge your issue. Treat your wound.

OPEN WOUNDS

In the Bible, the woman with the issue of blood only sought out help when she knew that she had an issue. She knew that something was wrong. She was bleeding and no one wanted to be around her. She was not supposed to go out in public in her condition but her desperation to stop bleeding on people was louder than the people judging her because of her issue.

Sometimes people don't get the help they need because they are afraid of how people will judge them and their issue. The primary reason people don't come up during altar calls is because they don't want their issue to be judged.

At some point, you have to break free of what you think other people are thinking and saying about you and be courageous enough to get what you need.

You need healing.

The journey to healing is a journey of courage. It takes courage to expose your wound and be healed. Sometimes, your desperation will drive you to do things that you have never seen done before – which also takes courage.

The woman with the issue of blood was desperate. She was at a place of despair. She had never seen Jesus heal anyone of her issue, but she reached her breaking point. She tried everything else, except Jesus.

It turned out that nothing else worked *but* Jesus.

Just because you haven't seen Jesus heal and perform in the way that you are seeking Him to perform, doesn't mean that He isn't able to do what you need Him to do. He may have chosen you to be the first.

Sometimes, Jesus will allow you to be in a desperate situation so that you can be an example for others of what He can do.

I've read this scripture several times, but while reading recently, I had to pause... and ask myself, *"Why was Jesus her last choice?"*

I began to think about our culture and society today. People are in pain. You can see it in their eyes, and you can hear it when they talk. Yet, the True Answer to their pain is often their last choice.

When you're in a painful situation, how long does it take you to reach for Jesus?

How long have you been bleeding?

How long do you reject your wound?

How long do you walk in denial of your condition?

The longer you walk in denial, the more *damage* you do – to yourself and to others.

Your pain becomes your comfort. It becomes familiar to you where anytime something goes right, you are quick to question it rather than accept it.

Consider this... what if the woman with the issue of blood would have reached out to Jesus sooner?

How many years would she have saved if she would have tried Jesus sooner?

How much more abundant would her life have been if she would have sought out Jesus sooner?

How many years, months, or days did she suffer unnecessarily?

How many people did she bleed on?

Over the years, I've noticed that there are several people who are in pain and despair but haven't reached for Jesus.

What if you sought Jesus the moment that you felt pain? Not just physical pain, but also emotional and mental pain.

Trust for America's Health reports the *Pain of the Nation* where they access the suicide rates as well as alcohol induced and drug overdose deaths. In 2021, the United States death rate due to alcohol, drugs, and suicide increased by 11%. Since then, those numbers continue to climb, which ultimately shows that people are hurting and attempting to cover their pain by going numb.

When you reject your wound, you reject The Answer.

Seeking Jesus can be uncomfortable when you're going through a tough time because, to receive healing, you must be willing to face your pain.

The longer you put seeking Jesus off, the longer you suffer unnecessarily and you will bleed on more people.

Sometimes desperation is necessary to gather enough courage and strength to seek God and be healed.

Don't walk in denial and delay the healing that you desperately need.

It's time to heal. And the first step to heal is to feel. HEAL Girl!

(Source: https://www.tfah.org/report-details/pain-in-the-nation-2023/).

OPEN WOUNDS

CHAPTER 3

Healed Vision

After I concluded my first year working in marketing, I reached a place where I earned enough money to have time to focus on me – more specifically my health.

I was working out daily, eating better, and after having a few health challenges in the past, my body was finally beginning to function the way that it was designed to function with little to no medication.

I took Christmas break to spend with my son as I have always done in previous years. While on Christmas break, I did what most adults who work do – I went to the doctor to have my annual physical and woman exam.

For my woman exam, I decided to visit an office that focused on all things concerning women. During my initial exam with my new gynecologist, she asked, *"Does anyone in your family have the BRACA gene?"*

I answered, *"I'm not sure. My maternal grandmother had breast cancer and underwent treatment."*

My doctor responded, *"How old was your grandmother when she was diagnosed?"*

I said, *"She was in her 60's or 70's."*

Immediately, my doctor exhaled and didn't seem as concerned. She assured me, *"Your grandmother probably didn't have the gene. It's normally a concern for younger women."*

She paused… *"Do you still want to take the test… just in case?"*

Not concerned that anything would be abnormal, I said, *"Sure."*

I took the blood test, then I left. When I got in my car, I called my mother just to double check about the BRACA gene. She quickly responded by saying no one in our family had the gene which strengthened my belief that this test was nothing to be concerned about.

Two weeks later, I returned to work from my Christmas vacation. I was home working while a technician finished setting up my new cable and internet services.

My phone rang and the call was from an unknown number. I normally don't answer unknown numbers, but I was feeling really refreshed from my break *and* I was very happy that my internet and cable services were being updated – so why not?

I answered the phone… but I was so unprepared for what I was about to hear. It's amazing that what we hear can ignite the very thing that we thought was dead in our lives.

In Ezekiel 37, Ezekiel had a vision. In his vision, God placed him in a valley that was full of dry bones. Ezekiel continues in saying that God led him all around the bones. Ezekiel couldn't deny what he was seeing and experiencing because it was God who placed him in it and led him through it.

HEALED VISION

Although the conditions were unpleasant, Ezekiel's eyes were wide open to what he was standing in. He was able to describe what he saw – accurately.

Are you able to describe what you see? Many times, we rely on what we feel. It may be easier to describe what's felt rather than what's seen however, in order to speak life into what's dead, you cannot rely on feelings and emotions. You must be able to clearly see the truth about your situation, then combat it with God's Truth – the Word of God.

Ezekiel was able to describe the multitude of what he was surrounded by, including its condition.

When you are in life changing situations, it's hard to look at what you want to deny or reject. But true change in your situation begins when you can accurately identify what you are standing in. You have to be able to face your truth so that you can give it to God.

First Peter chapter five and verse seven tells you to…

"cast all your cares on Him, because He cares about you."

In Matthew chapter 11 and verse 28, Jesus encourages you to…

"Come to Me, all of you who are weary and burdened, and I will give you rest."

Your cares are not meant to be carried. They're meant to be casted.

But to cast your cares on God, you must first know what you're casting – and not just at surface level. Cast ALL of your cares, not just a layer of it.

This is why many people become confused about their healing. They feel that they have completely let go of the issue by giving it to God but, in reality, you only gave God a piece of your issue because you only faced "a piece" of your issue.

God wants it all. He wants it all because He wants you to be healed. He wants you to prosper in every way. He wants you to be in

HEALED VISION

good health and for your whole life to go well.

Don't give God false truths. Open your eyes. Ask God for clear vision and allow Him to lead you. Let Him lead you in the dead areas of your life, because He wants to resurrect it.

God desires to resurrect what you want to reject.

Look at those places in your life that you have rejected. God wants to know, can what you see live again?

So, the question isn't *can* you be healed; The question is, do you *want* to be healed?

Cast your cares and let go of ALL of it. Be healed.

HEAL GIRL

CHAPTER 4
Heal the Unseen

I struggled with fear and anxiety for majority of my life. I remember I used to fake being sick so that I could stay home from school, if I knew that we were having a fire drill. The anticipation of waiting on the drill to happen made me sick. My focus was on the exact moment of when the alarm would sound.

I know this sounds silly, trivial, and even minimal but there was a deeper issue behind the fear and anxiety I experienced. The drill only triggered the *real* issue at hand.

I wasn't afraid of the sound or the drill. The real issue was that I wasn't controlling the drill. I had no control over what was happening, and I had to completely rely on whoever was running the drill. I didn't know the exact moment that they were pulling the drill and that gave me anxiety.

A lot of times we label anxiety and fear as the issue, when the true source behind anxiety is control.

Some Christians get frustrated when they've sacrificed for the sake of the gospel, carried their cross, evangelized, yet still are unable to escape tragedy in life.

Note: Be careful not to mistake your "works" for the kingdom as insurance against tragedy and calamity in life.

Jesus was the son of God and still had to relinquish His control to submit to God's will in the midst of pain.

Luke gives us an inside look to Jesus' pain that's seen through His conversation with God…

"Father, if you are willing, take this cup away from me – nevertheless, not my will, but yours, be done." (Luke 22:42)

Jesus had the ability to control what was going to happen in His life, but His submission to God was a safer place.

I often controlled and manipulated situations in my life, and when things couldn't be controlled, my response was fear and anxiety.

Over the years through therapy and much prayer and fasting, I was able to conquer the spirit of fear. I learned how to cope with what I couldn't control and really rest in God.

But when I received the call regarding the results from my blood test, my body froze in fear. My mind resorted to denial in response to fear.

Not knowing who was calling, I answered, *"Hello?"*

The person on the other end responded, *"Hello, this is 'Sue'. I am one of the patient counselors here at [the company who processed the test]."*

I signaled the representative who was at my home working on my cable and internet letting him know that I needed to take the call. Then I returned to the call and said, *"Oh hi Sue. How are you?"*

Sue replied, *"I'm well, thanks for asking! What about you?"*

I said happily, *"I'm great, thank you."*

Mind you, it didn't click that she was a patient counselor. In my mind, I was still expecting everything to be normal because there was no reason for it not to be.

I was in my thriving and winning season, plus I didn't have a family history that would put me at risk for the test to come back positive.

Sue continued, *"Uh, Tiffany – do you have a minute?"*

I said, *"Yes."*

Sue said, *"I'm calling you regarding your results from the blood test that you took 2 weeks ago. Are you driving?"*

"No, I'm home," I replied.

Sue continued, *"Okay. Good news is you don't have the BRACA gene. However, your test came back positive for another gene which puts you at a significantly higher risk to develop cancer."*

I paused and stared out my window. I slowly made my way to my desk to sit down, and I rested my head on my fist.

It felt like someone knocked the wind out of me. I was the healthiest that I had ever been in my adult life, and *now this?*

Surely this lady called the wrong person. There is no way. No one in my family has it and God, you chose me to have this?

These were some of the racing thoughts that I had in that moment that were interrupted by, *"Tiffany? Tiffany? Honey, are you there?"*

I snapped out of it and said, *"Yes, I'm here… okay."*

Sue asked, *"Are you okay?"*

I replied, *"I'm trying to be."*

Sue responded, *"This is a lot. Do you want to take a moment to process, and we reconnect later?"*

I said, *"No, you're fine… what does all of this mean?"*

Sue went down a list of organs that are directly affected from the syndrome, which would require me to get multiple procedures and tests done annually to ensure that there isn't a trace of cancer in my body; or that *if* a trace was found, they'd be able to catch and treat it early.

This was something that I could not control. As a result, the anxiety that I thought I was healed from, began rearing its head little by little; and instead of facing the anxiety by addressing it, I denied it, called it the devil, and kept moving – wounded.

Sometimes the roots of the strongmen or struggles that you have are much greater than what you are willing to address.

Most trees are beautiful. If nurtured and cared for correctly, they grow into this big, beautiful plant that has many purposes for life and our environment – all of which begins with just a seed.

A seed is small but has everything it needs to begin new life – including roots. Once the seed begins to grow, the first part of it that breaks through its coat are the roots. The roots break through and begin growing downward and become an anchor for the new plant.

Every new growth in your life – good or bad – has an anchor. It has a root. It becomes a part of your core. Most times, when going through the healing process, people only trim what can be seen; and when you start to look better and get compliments from others about how well you *look*, you prematurely exit the healing process, and the root of your struggle remains.

Often, this goes unnoticed until life becomes difficult and you begin to feel the pressure from whatever is troubling you. When the fire of life gets turned up, then the core of who you are is activated – including your struggle (that is, if you didn't uproot it).

You can continue to cut the branches of your struggle and even stop feeding it; but unless you completely uproot it, that struggle will always be present in your life.

Although a tree comes from one seed and one trunk, it has many roots.

It's not the branches (or what's obvious) of your struggle that causes you to fall. What causes you to fall are the things that are found beneath the soil and are buried in your heart.

Your struggle has many roots, and you have to be willing and committed to the process to take the time to address them all.

HEAL THE UNSEEN

All things can be uprooted but you must be willing to take the time to trace the source of your struggle so that you can uproot it completely.

You will feel relief from uprooting one root, but you will experience freedom from uprooting all roots.

Freedom is your portion. You just have to prioritize time for you to HEAL Girl!

HEAL GIRL

CHAPTER 5

The Key to a Healed Identity

In 2005, two days before my birthday, my boyfriend made a visit to my parents' home. I had just started college and began working with a very reputable company. My boyfriend and I had been dating for a little over 2 years. He spent a lot of time over my parents' house (even when I wasn't there); so it wasn't out of the ordinary for him to make unexpected visits. Only this time he stopped by when I was asleep.

He came in my room and woke me up. I'm a person who has always valued sleep. So in the past, I was normally unpleasant when someone woke me up from my deep sleep. But when I saw it was him, I was unusually happy – I was so in love!

He was kneeling by my bed, but I still managed to greet him with a huge hug.

Then I asked him, *"What are you doing here?"*

He looked at me and then reached in his pocket to grab a box. He opened it, then asked, *"Will you marry me?"*

I was completely surprised (which is hard to do), and so happy. I took a deep breath, threw my hands up in excitement and said *"YES!"*

He smiled. Took the ring out and placed it on my finger. It was a beautiful, NICE rock. We embraced, talked for a little, then he left.

The next morning, reality hit…

"I got to tell my parents…"

My heart dropped. I knew that they loved my fiancé, but I also knew that they weren't expecting me to leave the nest so soon. Although we were more mature than most teenagers, we were still so young.

Nonetheless, I knew that I still had to tell them… so I started plotting.

THE KEY TO A HEALED IDENTITY

I'm a Daddy's girl, so I knew that it would be easier to tell him. Then, I could leave it to him to tell my mom and the rest of my family.

I placed my ring back in its box and began walking towards my parent's room. I peeked through the doorway and saw my Dad with his glasses on lying on his stomach on his bed. He was preparing a sermon. I took a deep breath and walked in.

"Hey Daddy."

He looked up, smiled, and said, *"Hey baby! What's up?"*

I handed him the box with my ring in it.

Completely taken by surprise, his whole expression changed. He said, *"What's that?"*

I said, *"It's a ring,"* I opened it, *"See?"*

"A ring for what??" He asked.

Knees shaking, I said, *"I'm getting married."*

He asked, *"To who?"*

He already knew, but I still told him since he asked.

He finally worked through the shock and said, *"Slow your roll."*

Before I move forward with this chapter, I just want you to know that I was literally laughing out loud as I was writing this.

Looking back, I can see how immature I was and how much I wasn't ready for something as big as marriage.

I struggled with telling one of the people who I trusted the most, which showed that I had a huge struggle with fear and rejection – which is linked to insecurity.

At that time, I felt like my dreams were coming true. I was marrying the man of my dreams, but I still struggled with being *"good enough."*

THE KEY TO A HEALED IDENTITY

"Is this good enough for Daddy's approval?"

My identity wasn't solid at all because the decisions I made for *my* life were still trapped in my thoughts of what other people would think of me.

This is a prison that many people, more specifically adults, still struggle with today. With the culture and social media being rooted on what the world thinks of you, you can easily get entangled into the trap of your identity being wrapped up in the world versus wrapped up in God.

But this is how our adversary works. The devil is often referred to as a serpent in the Bible. When Jesus was giving instruction to the disciples on how to navigate in this world, He told them…

""Look, I'm sending you out like sheep among wolves. Therefore be as shrewd as serpents and as innocent as doves." (Matthew 10:16 CSB)

Another translation says to be as *wise* as serpents. Serpents are wise because despite not having what most have (hands, feet, legs, arms, etc.), they are still able to accomplish their goals in this world.

The devil doesn't have what we have, yet he is still able to deceive. He deceives us in really sly ways, such as highlighting temptations that would nurture identity theft in a culture. People are falling into this trap and losing sight of their identity – which leads to them losing their security in God.

It's so simple and most people don't see this as a big deal – but that's how deception works.

"It's not a big deal."

At that moment, it may not be a big deal from a natural standpoint, but how is this affecting you spiritually? Do you see yourself worthy to be a child of God? Or are you tiptoeing around your Heavenly Father because you are unsure if He approves of your actions?

THE KEY TO A HEALED IDENTITY

Truth is, He may not like what you're doing. But here's the good news! He's already provided a way for you to receive total healing in the area that you are afraid of presenting to Him.

Healing is available to you. There's no need to tiptoe around a God Who already knows and has the antidote to your struggle.

The longer you hide, the longer you will feel trapped in your mind and in your heart. You will continue to walk around discontent, unsatisfied, and unfulfilled. There is no task or project that you can do that will cover or fill the void that only God can heal.

God wants to heal you. He wants to mend your heart. He wants you to have peace. He wants you to laugh again. He wants you to find security in Him.

But you have to slow down and get to know Him. God is not a fairytale. He desires to rescue you. But you have to be still long enough to learn His desires for you. You learn God's desires for you by learning His character.

There's a more rewarding life waiting for you; and you don't have to wait to get to Heaven to experience it. Freedom can be yours today.

So, take the time to slow your roll so that you can HEAL Girl!

Slowing your roll means to slow your pace on things that you are currently doing. To do so, you must properly prioritize things so that you don't miss a beat. Prioritizing your healing is one of the best things that you can do for yourself. What are some things that you can begin doing <u>today</u> to prioritize your healing? For example: finding a Christian counselor, choosing to get up an hour early to spend time with God, having the necessary conversations with unresolved relationships, apologizing, etc.

THE KEY TO A HEALED IDENTITY

Whatever you decide, list it below along with a *trusted* accountability partner who will support you in keeping your commitment. (*Tip: An accountability partner is not a "Yes Man."*)

_____
_____
_____
_____
_____
_____
_____
_____
_____
_____
_____
_____
_____
_____
_____
_____
_____
_____
_____
_____

HEAL GIRL

THE KEY TO A HEALED IDENTITY

CHAPTER 6

Your Truth Uncovered

"Do not be afraid of their faces, For I am with you to deliver you," says the Lord."
Jeremiah 1:8 NKJV

This was the Lord's response to Jeremiah after Jeremiah doubted what God said about Him.

God was clear to Jeremiah about his purpose. He confirmed His plans to Jeremiah by saying,

""Before I formed you in the womb I knew you; Before you were born I sanctified you; I ordained you a prophet to the nations.""
Jeremiah 1:5 NKJV

It wasn't by surprise what God created Jeremiah to do. God already had in mind Jeremiah's purpose before Jeremiah was conceived. Before Jeremiah took his first breath, God already prepared and knitted His purpose into Jeremiah to be a prophet to nations. Jeremiah had everything he needed.

Jeremiah's life was significant to God. It was special. So, God shared His plans with Jeremiah when he was old enough to understand because there was a need for what He placed in Jeremiah.

I'm a prophet. It's something that I knew of ever since I was a teenager. Before I knew God graced me to be a Pastor, I knew that God called me to be prophet. I didn't know I would be a minister (and eventually Pastor) until I was an adult – but a prophet? God revealed that to me as a child.

However, I didn't have clear understanding of what being a prophet meant. I grew up in a Baptist church and didn't shift to Pentecostal until I was nearly an adult. Even still, prophecy wasn't as common as it is now. So as far as I knew, prophecy was just revealing the future. I only had a surface level understanding of it.

HEAL GIRL

In my teenage years, I began getting called out in services. I was very strong willed and at one point I was tired of getting called out and ended up walking out of churches before altar calls so that I would avoid all eyes being on me. But God knew His daughter. He would send His Word in the middle of services or at rehearsals — times when I didn't expect it. So I couldn't run.

I would receive Words that confirmed what the Lord already shared with me.

You are God's chosen.
There is something special about you.
God is going to use you in a different way — for your generation.
The Holy Ghost is heavy on your life.
You are God's Prophet of time.
God has given you the ability to feel what He feels.

These were rich words that, most times, I didn't operate in because I had the same concerns as Jeremiah — I cannot speak! I'm only a youth!

YOUR TRUTH UNCOVERED

When children are born, they have no fear. We are created fearless, which is why we have to learn about danger. Before being told about danger, danger wasn't even a thought in our minds.

So, why would Jeremiah, me, and possibly you, have a thought that people wouldn't listen to us because of our age or whatever inadequacy you're placing before God?

What formed that perception in your mind and fear in your heart that you aren't heard? What makes you doubt God – the most trusted individual that you know; the One who created you? Why is there still doubt in your heart even after He affirmed that He created and prepared you just for this?

Your perceptions and mind battles are developed from what you see growing up. In my case, I never saw prophecy in real life, and I was taught that what I saw on television was staged and fake. I didn't know of any prophets in my family. So how could I operate in something that wasn't common in my bloodline and immediate surroundings?

Not only was it not common, but in most cases, it was rejected. So it was foreign to me and *if* I accepted it, it would lead to another level of rejection in my life.

This was the mind battle that stopped me from accepting what the Lord created and called me to do.

If you are called and chosen by God, most times He will give you the assignment to be the difference. He will call you to the unknown. He will call you to unfamiliar territory because of the need that is in your family, community, and ultimately the world. He called you because He knew that He would have your attention to work through you.

What in your life has shaped your doubts around what God called you to do? It's time to identify and uproot them. It's not cute to deny the powerful call on your life and disguise it as humility and modesty. That's the enemy deceiving you. God called you to be as bold as a Lion because people are waiting to receive what God placed on the inside of you. You can't tiptoe around it. You have to own it.

Your inadequacy doesn't cancel what God has already placed in you; but it may cause a delay because to fully operate in your calling, you must overcome the battle in your mind and realize that you're worthy of the calling. Your calling is a part of His plan. It's intentional.

The Bible tells us in Corinthians that we all have treasures in earthen vessels — meaning that we carry something special within our natural bodies. It's supernatural. It's a treasure — in other words, it's hidden.

Everyone can't see it. You may not even see it; BUT you know it's there, and God knows it's there because He placed it there. Once you become aware of what you carry, God will present opportunities for you to walk in what you carry.

Many people do not walk in power, authority, and dominion because they doubt how others would receive the treasure that God placed within them. So, they ignore the God-given opportunities to reveal the treasure.

What you carry is not for you. It's for the opportunities God places before you.

Your old belief system has expired. It's time to develop and nurture a new one that is conducive to what God created you to do.

Let go of old belief systems and the perceptions of others because people are waiting on you to HEAL Girl!

Jeremiah had doubts around what God created him to do — but here's the game changer…

He presented his doubts to God — not people. When God has called you to do something out of the ordinary, you can't invite everyone in with the expectation of them understanding it and giving you their full support. Sometimes God callings are bigger than what people can understand, and they won't understand it until they see it in operation.

You can't share it with everyone, especially if you are still unsure about it. But there will be some people you can trust who will ignite you into your purpose, but it will take God leading you to the right people.

I want you to take a moment to identify every doubt that you have about your calling or something that you know that God wants you to do. Write down those thoughts in the section below. Then, I want you to go a step further and identify WHY you have those doubts. Identifying the reason behind your behavior uproots the doubt as a whole, so that it never returns.

Once you uproot it, then search the scripture for Truth relating to your calling or assignment. Or Truth of what God thinks about you. Write it down! By doing so, you are now planting good seed in place of the uprooted doubt.

HEAL GIRL

YOUR TRUTH UNCOVERED

CHAPTER 7

Voice Triggers

When I was a young girl, I hated being in trouble. As a matter of fact, when my siblings got in trouble, I fled to a "safe place" until the coast was clear. My parents weren't violent or physically abusive; my fleeing was solely because I hated to see them disappointed and upset.

Like most, we would always know when we were in trouble because instead of my parents calling us by our nicknames, they would call us by our full name. For me, it was just "Tiffany".

When I became an adult, I didn't detach the fear of being in trouble from being called by my name —Tiffany. So whenever an older adult called me "Tiffany" instead of "Tiff", it triggered me and I froze. I immediately resorted back to the little girl who was afraid of being disliked or unaccepted because of something that I did wrong.

It wasn't until I began counseling that I dealt with the root of that trigger and was able to overcome it. Counseling didn't focus on the trigger or the effect it had on me, but my counselor analyzed my relationships and how they affected my behavior. My relationships created roots in my life that stunted my growth emotionally.

I had to have difficult conversations with key relationships in my life (including my family) to address the "voice trigger" and all of my immature behaviors. It was difficult because I never wanted to hurt, disappoint, or even be misunderstood by the ones I loved; which is why I had the trigger in the first place — hearing my full name, "Tiffany", meant that I disappointed someone.

It was a hard pill to swallow. I knew that after having these conversations, it was highly likely that I would be misunderstood and potentially disappoint or hurt them… but at the end of it all, I would be free. I also knew that, eventually, my freedom would help them thrive in life.

Today, I'm standing on the other side of this and I can tell you that this stands true – my freedom is now helping those I love.

To help those you love, you must make a decision to keep your heart pure in the midst of being misunderstood. It's very easy to cut people off completely when you have been hurt by them. It's a natural reflex but it's not biblical.

Joseph was betrayed by his brothers and endured years of being wrongfully accused and forgotten. When he became free and was living in the promise of God, he invited his brothers and father to live in God's promise with him (after being petty for a moment).

You have to do what's necessary to be healed. It's not in God's will for everyone to travel with you on your healing journey, but it may be in His will for them to share in God's promise for you – in His timing. What you do after you're free matters.

VOICE TRIGGERS

Now sometimes you will need to set up boundaries for people who just don't mean you any good. But even then, you're not cutting them off. You're just being wise with who you give access to. In this case, you'd be protecting your promise. You protect the promise when you protect your heart. You can't protect your promise with a bitter and angry heart. Bitterness and anger perverts your vision. It taints your discernment which could lead to you giving the wrong person boundaries.

You have to keep your heart pure so that, if necessary, you will be able to invite others into God's promise with you — no matter how much they hurt you.

It's hard to make choices that you know are best for you but, in that moment, may hurt someone else. Everyone won't be happy with your steps to freedom initially. But eventually they will appreciate the steps that you chose to take because they'll benefit from it. Not only will they see that you are better, but they'll also become better from you being free.

It takes bold moves to be the difference. To be the light of change, you have to be different. To disrupt cycles and old behaviors, you have to be different. You have to be okay with being different. Different isn't bad. In order to be a light in the midst of darkness, you must stand out.

And yes — people will misunderstand your light; that is, until they see that you're able to lead them out of the cave of darkness.

Leaders must be lights. You have to be able to see before you can lead. And don't get comfortable with being the only light. Help others to become lights — lead them to healing.

Your light heals others. Don't prematurely walk out of your healing process because your light is rejected. Your light will naturally expose their darkness. It's natural to be rejected in the healing process — so don't eject from the process just because you're rejected.

VOICE TRIGGERS

Your healing is necessary not only for you, but for those around you. It is my prayer that you don't escape the process due to the discomfort and voices from people. Your healing is worth them rejecting and misunderstanding you. Don't allow the enemy to distract you and pull you from the healing that's necessary in your life.

Stay committed — for you.
Stay anchored — for you.
Stay focused — for you.
Stay prayerful — for you.
Stay accountable — for you.
Stay humble — for you.

It's not selfish to do all of these things for you because YOU are a part of a greater vision that affects others. So do what you need to do for you, so that you can be better for them.

Uproot what triggers you and do what's necessary for you to HEAL Girl!

HEAL GIRL

CHAPTER 8

God's Reminder

One morning, I laid in my bed (under the cover) not wanting to start my day. God led me to my own podcast. As I looked at my episode stats, *"Help! I feel ugly!"* was the episode with the most listens. So, I decided to listen.

I was in one of the ugliest seasons of my life and was feeling really ugly — not physically, but emotionally. I was just sick and tired of where I was in life.

I was tired of struggling, and tired of being sick. I was tired of being single and feeling overlooked. I was just tired of repeating the cycle of this daily. These were all feelings that I harbored. I concealed how I felt so that I could get through my day — repeating the cycle.

HEAL GIRL

In 1 Kings 19, God had just used Elijah mightily. God performed a miracle on his behalf which led people to believing in God. However, after the miracle was done and God was done "moving", Elijah found himself running for his life.

He was tired of running and told the LORD that he had enough. Then, he asked God to take his life. Shortly after, he fell asleep in that same place. As a response, God sent an angel who woke him up, gave him food and water, and told him to eat or the journey would be too much for him.

Elijah slept at the place where he gave up and instead of God leaving him there, he sent what Elijah needed and reminded him of the journey ahead.

Just because you give up emotionally, doesn't cancel the journey that God has laid out before you. God will meet you where you're at to awaken you and give you exactly what you need to go on.

GOD'S REMINDER

When I recorded this episode, I thought it was one of the worst episodes that I recorded. So, I was surprised to see that it had turned out to be the most popular episode. After listening to it, I understand why — the anointing was all over this episode. This was God's reminder to me.

Listening to it awakened me from a place where I was becoming numb, to a place where I felt refreshed and revived. God's reminder resurrected me.

When the angel appeared to Elijah, there wasn't any thunder, and he didn't shake Elijah silly until he woke up. The Bible says that the angel suddenly "touched" him. God's reminders are not always loud. I have found that when you're in a sensitive spot like this, you can't handle the "loud". But God will meet you in your frustration and "touch" you subtly to remind you of your journey ahead.

He will send you what you need to sooth your anger, disappointment, and discouragement and give you the strength to move on.

HEAL GIRL

Life can bring a lot of discomfort and weight where you won't have a desire to move to your next; but you can't stay asleep forever. Your journey is too important. There are too many people in your pipeline who are waiting to see God's glory through you.

Seeing how many times it was downloaded, showed me that people all over this world struggle with the same thing. Ugly feelings. It's common.

However, if you open yourself up to God (even in your frustration), He has a way of getting through to you — even in your sleep. In times where you may feel useless and not effective, God will send special reminders to show you how special you really are. He will show you that you are chosen for the journey you're on.

I'm going to keep this chapter brief because I want to give you an opportunity to listen to this episode. It says it all. There's nothing that I need to add to it.

Scan the code to listen…

GOD'S REMINDER

HEAL GIRL

CHAPTER 9

Familiar Ground

My mom is a registered nurse. When my siblings and I were younger, she worked long shifts in the pediatric intensive care unit at a local hospital. One of her coworkers had a pool and offered to give me and my siblings swimming lessons. When my mom came home and shared this information with us, we all rejoiced at the thought of being able to get in a pool.

We lived in the acreage in West Palm Beach, Florida and, at the time, the closest thing we had to a pool was our pond in our backyard. So, to be able to get in water versus only being by the water to go fishing, was a big deal for us.

To prepare for our swimming lessons, my mom took us to the store to get new bathing suits. We were so excited. We left the store with new bathing suits, and my sister and I left with new rubber swimming caps. My sister and I had very long hair and my mom didn't want our hair to become damaged by the chlorine or dried out by the constant washing… not to mention how tired she'd be from washing and doing our hair after every lesson.

We arrived at our first lesson. The lady's pool was screened in which was great because we didn't have to fight with bugs or lizards. We all got in the water and the first thing the woman taught us was how to hold our breath underwater. My brother and sister did it with ease. I was a little apprehensive and cautious. So, I did it little by little.

While I was taking baby steps on how to go underwater, my brother was learning the correct way to swim versus fighting the water, and my sister was learning how to let go and float on her back. Although swimming was the goal, floating on your back seemed so much more relaxing than what I saw my brother doing.

FAMILIAR GROUND

So, after I conquered going underwater, I asked our teacher if she could teach me how to do what my sister was doing. Of course, she said yes.

I was so excited… that is, until I realized that I had to let go of the control that I had in the water to successfully float. I attempted to float for the remainder of the lesson but every time my feet left the ground, I panicked and could not relax enough to float.

I had to let go of what I knew and trust that the water would carry me. But I couldn't let go.

The very moment I realized that my feet were no longer touching the bottom of the pool, it didn't matter how well I was floating; all I could think about was sinking because of the depth of the water.

Healing requires walking in faith. Walking in faith requires that you release what you *can* control so that you, and those who are watching you, can experience the miracle of God.

HEAL GIRL

God still works miracles; but it's often our desire to hold on to what we can control, which keeps those miracles from manifesting in our lives.

Wanting to always have control is an outward display of doubt and disbelief. You feel like you have to do it or else it won't happen — that's disbelief.

In Matthew 13, Jesus was teaching powerfully from a boat using parables so that those who stood on the shore listening could easily understand. At the conclusion of Him teaching, He asked everyone if they understood all that He taught (what a great leadership technique modeled out!). They answered, "Yes."

He left there, returned to His hometown and began teaching there; but received a different response from those in His hometown. They were unable to receive Jesus' wisdom and miracles because they couldn't get past who they knew Him to be naturally — Mary and a carpenter's son.

FAMILIAR GROUND

They relied on their knowledge and missed the miracle. They missed the very thing that could have helped them, all because they couldn't get past what they knew about Jesus' history. What they knew about Jesus naturally, fueled their unbelief.

As a result, Jesus didn't do many miracles there because of their unbelief.

Healing and miracles are supernatural. In order to experience them, you must let go of what you know and find peace in God. Rest in His Word so that you can receive what He wants for you in that moment.

I could not swim because I knew, at some point, my feet would no longer touch the ground unless I went underwater. The deeper I went, the less safe I felt because I couldn't control it.

When seeking healing, emotionally or naturally, you must not be afraid to go deeper. The deeper you go the less you're able to control; but it's at that point that healing begins to manifest and the supernatural is activated.

You have to be committed to let go of what you know so that you can rest in capable arms — the arms of God. In the arms of God lies miracles and healing, and to access it you have to release what you know and silence your doubt and disbelief.

Jesus wanted to do miracles but people in His hometown were very familiar with Him. Familiarity kills promises. It blinds you from seeing the truth about what God wants for you. It blocks you from experiencing the freedom behind letting go of what has been known or familiar to you.

The ground was familiar to me, but freedom was found in going deep and letting go. I didn't have to worry about sinking because God equipped me to swim in the deep.

God has equipped you to swim into the deep, but you have to let go of what has been a familiar place to you.

FAMILIAR GROUND

Your healing is in deep waters and God is there waiting for you. The ground that you are so desperately holding on to may be keeping you from experiencing God's best. God's best is often found in deep waters.

What is God's best for you? God's best is not obtainable in our own strength. His best is often a miracle or brought to you supernaturally, and accessed by faith.

Experience the freedom that's yours by choosing to let go of the ground you're on.

HEAL Girl! Because that familiar place has expired.

What has been your "ground"? Is God nudging you to let go and leave the "ground" you have known? Grounds will keep you bound because of the safety that it promises. But your freedom is worth letting go of what you have known. Freedom may seem risky because it's unfamiliar in many ways, but it's necessary and worth it. To receive God's promises and blessings in their totality, you must be free.

In the space below, write down what your "ground" is. Then look at what you've written down, and decide today that you're going to leave that familiar ground so that you can walk in freedom.

_____
_____
_____
_____
_____
_____
_____
_____
_____
_____
_____
_____
_____
_____
_____

FAMILIAR GROUND

HEAL GIRL

CHAPTER 10

Let Go of Old Patterns

"Stay in the forward fight. Forget those things—ways, thought patterns, behaviors—of the past. What God has for you is yet before you—in front of you. Proper desperation is the breeding ground for miracles. Misplaced desperation breeds messes... poor choices & unwanted consequences."

This was part of a text that my mentor sent to me. I was in a very interesting season of my life.

I was in (what we like to call) my winning season. From the outside, God was blessing my son and I tremendously. I was in a place where doors were wide open. If I thought it, then I could literally have it. Prayers were being answered and God was doing amazing things in my life. He was doing things that left me speechless and with the thought, "Did this really just happen?"

I didn't have need for anything – yet, I wanted something so desperately, and I was becoming frustrated and impatient.

I was single and I felt like I had been single long enough. It was time for me to meet my man. I longed for the opportunity to share my highs and lows with him. I longed to grow with him and to enjoy life together. I longed for companionship, and it didn't seem like the person that God had set aside for me would appear anytime soon.

So, I struggled… and in my struggle I contemplated settling. My patience grew short, and thoughts of compromise began to settle in. I wanted to experience the prophecy that I received from several different, trusted individuals. I wanted God to deliver me from the season that I was in so that I could live in my promised season.

But who says that your promised season isn't now?

LET GO OF OLD PATTERNS

In Isaiah 43, this is what the Lord says…

"… 'Do not fear, for I have redeemed you; I have called you by your name; you are mine. When you pass through the waters, I will be with you, and the rivers will not overwhelm you. When you walk through the fire, you will not be scorched, and the flame will not burn you.'" (Isaiah 43:1-2 CSB)

God didn't say that He would deliver us from unpleasant conditions, but instead He reassured us that we would not be consumed in it.

There are seasons where God *will* deliver you, but there are also seasons where you must draw close to what God has supplied and navigate through the discomfort. The discomfort that you feel is developing you so that you can thrive in your promised season.

God is birthing a new season through your endurance. Do you not perceive it?

"Look, I am about to do something new; even now it is coming. Do you not see it? Indeed, I

will make a way in the wilderness, rivers in the desert." (Isaiah 43:19 CSB)

He's not taking you out of the wilderness; He's making a way in the wilderness so that you can walk through. The way that He is making is *"something new."* He's not taking you out of the desert; He's providing water so that you can endure your desert season. The river that He is providing is *"something new."*

I often wondered why God asked the question, *"Do you not perceive it?"* in this scripture; and I've found that it's because many times we look for deliverance when God is releasing provision.

You miss the provision because you doubt your ability to thrive in discomfort. You miss the provision because you become frustrated with not being delivered.

Dissatisfaction and discontent can keep you from realizing the truth of what's in front of you.

LET GO OF OLD PATTERNS

What God is providing in your rough season is unheard of. Finding an uncovered path in the wilderness is uncommon, *and* you don't find rivers in a desert. But with God, you can have access to that. God provides what is uncommon and unimagined.

A river is moving water – meaning that it is always drawing from the source. So, although your conditions may be uncomfortable, you have been given what you need to survive your tough season.

I didn't fully acknowledge this at the time because I was overwhelmed with loneliness and despair. God was blessing my socks off, but I was losing hope that a "husband" was a part of God's plan for me.

It was an interesting season because of how unsettled my mind was.

Two days prior to receiving this text, I had dinner with my mentor, and we had a very in-depth conversation about my frustrations. She listened closely. She validated feelings that were not harmful to my future and heard the sentiments of my heart. I shared with her that at times, I felt that I was operating in behaviors of my past because I was becoming hopeless in this journey.

"Forget those things—ways, thought patterns, behaviors—of the past."

As long as we remember the past, we will operate in the past. Your thoughts can keep you wounded. It can keep you unproductive. It can keep you fearful, angry, frustrated and ultimately dissatisfied.

There is a reason that God instructed Lot and his family not to look back on Sodom and Gomorrah. He was destroying their past and everything that it encompassed for a reason; because the moment you look back on it is the moment that you are no longer looking at what's ahead of you – your future.

You want to be delivered? Give your past to God and forget it. Your past no longer serves you. Break up with your old ways and behaviors because it won't serve the people

LET GO OF OLD PATTERNS

and things that are in your new season – the old doesn't have purpose in a new season.

If you want to break out in the new, then you have to break up with the old. Don't miss the new that God is bringing in your life because you're stuck in old ways, behaviors, and thoughts. Your old thoughts will not serve you in this new season.

Cycles rely on thought patterns. What are you thinking? In this moment, ask God to reveal the thoughts that keep you from experiencing His new for you. Once He reveals them, say this:

"God I give you this thought: [say your old thought]. Please destroy it. I cast down every imagination and proud thing that was connected to this thought, and take it captive to obey Christ, according to 2 Corinthians 10:4-5. I choose to think on things that are true, honorable, just, pure, lovely, excellent, commendable, and praiseworthy, according to Philippians 4:8. Thank You for the new path and new ways that You have set before

me. I declare that I am walking in it and I won't look back. In Jesus' Name, amen."

LET GO OF OLD PATTERNS

CHAPTER 11

Control + Alt + Delete

My son had just started middle school and I just started a new job in marketing. Within months, I was promoted and when the number of tasks began to grow, the company began to grow with the hope that no one would become overwhelmed or burned out.

However, I had a hard time delegating tasks to others on the team. Often, we would get projects with little notice which would require new team members to complete new tasks in a very short period of time. We created processes that could teach anyone how to do the task step-by-step, but I was still uncomfortable with delegating tasks.

I wanted it done right. So as a result, I would decide to do some of the harder tasks for projects and give the easier tasks to the new team members to ease them in. However, this also became unproductive. The new team members weren't learning at the rate they needed and wanted to learn, *and* I became overwhelmed.

The answer to my problem was simple — let go and delegate. It was simple but I had an issue with letting go because I was still operating in perfection. I struggled with the thought that a lot of people struggle with: *"It won't be done right unless I do it."*

Which is so untrue. There are people who are capable of doing what you do. You just have to let go, have patience, and trust their learning process. We had to make mistakes to get to where we're at; so it's our responsibility to give others that same grace.

Because truth is, you can't do it all. You need help and you'll only receive help when you learn to let go and trust those who are capable of helping you.

Growing up, we had one windows computer. Everyone in the house used it, even my grandmother from time to time. We installed games and programs on it and once we got

AOL (aka the internet), the sky was the limit as to what we could access and download.

After a while, the computer wasn't as fast as it was when we first got it. It would freeze and stall on one screen a lot. When it froze, we just manually turned it off, and then back on again. Eventually, this became a pain in the neck, especially if the computer froze while we were on the internet. Not only did we have to wait for the computer to reboot, but once rebooted, we had to wait for our AOL dial up internet to reconnect.

Then, we found a quicker way to reset the computer without turning it off — Control + Alt + Delete. When we pressed those buttons together, it would command the computer to bring us back to the Windows login screen which automatically terminated the task that was causing the computer to freeze. Once on the login screen, it gave you the option to shut down or restart the computer the right way versus manually. It was a quick reset, without completely resetting the computer and losing everything that you were working on.

CONTROL + ALT + DELETE

Once we found this out, we used that command all of the time. Now that we had a quick way to get out of frozen or stalling situations, we downloaded more software.

We thought that we could give the computer more being that we had a quick way to exit and terminate tasks when they became too much.

Listen girl... as women we are very strong; but don't get so caught up in your strength and capacity to do things, that you end up taking on too much. You are not a superhero. You cannot do it all. Your strength is not there to be maxed out, it's to be used with wisdom — with strength to spare.

God is the Master of delegation. The only reason we have purpose in His Kingdom is because He delegated purpose to us.

Jesus shared this with His disciples...

"All things have been entrusted to me by my Father. No one knows the Son except the Father, and no one knows the Father except

the Son and anyone to whom the Son desires to reveal him. "Come to me, all of you who are weary and burdened, and I will give you rest. Take my yoke upon you and learn from me, because I am lowly and humble in heart, and you will find rest for your souls. For my yoke is easy and my burden is light.""
Matthew 11:27-30 CSB

God entrusted ALL THINGS to Jesus. And Jesus reveals these things to who He trusts. Once He reveals things to us, it may be a lot, which is why He says, Come to Me and learn from Me. Jesus reveals with the plan to teach us as we go.

We don't have to be overwhelmed with what He initially reveals to us. He wants us to come and rest in Him so that He can teach us step-by-step how to accomplish what's before us.

Perfectionism will always cause chaos. Why? Because you're not perfect. When you operate in perfectionism, you are choosing to operate in something that is unobtainable. It's a trick from the enemy that often stems back to an instance in your childhood where you thought you had to be perfect.

Perfectionism is not attainable. It will cause anxiety, overwhelm, racing thoughts, panic attacks, depression, worry, and eventually sickness. It wears down your body and is the opposite of what Jesus wants for you. Jesus wants you to rest from the chaos. Jesus is saying, "Come to the secret place and learn from Me."

We learn how to thrive in life by living in God's secret place (aka by making it a priority to spend intentional time with God).

Doing things right all of the time is not the way to living a free life. It's bondage. Learning is the way to freedom. The more you learn, the more you uproot the chaos out of your life.

I had to do a Control + Alt + Delete and learn that I could not do it all. And by accepting that truth, I embraced delegating to others and therefore embraced peace.

You don't have to be perfect to delegate or learn. But you do have to trust; and the place of learning must be a proven safe place where learning is easy.

Taking on too much in life will freeze your progression. Whenever it feels like you are stagnant, evaluate what's on your plate. Then perform a real-life Control + Alt + Delete. Start fresh and decide what tasks you can move off your plate and give to someone else. Who would be trustworthy to carry out that task with excellence?

Follow Jesus' model. He doesn't reveal what the Father delegated to Him to everyone. The Bible says that Jesus reveals to whom He desires to reveal those things to. The person whom you delegate to, must be trustworthy of that task to ensure that it will be done, not perfectly, but with excellence (there's a difference and the difference is worth noting).

When you have unrealistic desires of perfection, then you put that bondage on those who are helping you. However, when your standard is excellence, the expectation becomes attainable for your team. They're able to use their gifts without the weight of being perfect which will drive passion and increase the momentum to go over and beyond — producing excellence.

After I learned the art of letting go and delegating, I learned to use the strength that I had to spare to empower my team members based on the potential that they carried. It was a sweet spot and brought a lot of value to the company.

If you are reading this book, you are a leader in some capacity of your life. How are you leading? What do you need to let go of to ensure that those you're leading are benefiting from a healthy relationship?

Don't delay of uprooting what may be stunting your growth and progression. Lives depend on it. Take a moment to do a Control + Alt + Delete to find out what you can let go of to lead a healthier life.

HEAL GIRL

HEAL Girl! by saying goodbye to overwhelm and anxiety and saying hello to peace and productivity.

CONTROL + ALT + DELETE

CHAPTER 12

Heal Preacher

Daily, I see powerful men and women of God give revelation on Facebook that only justifies the pain that they are feeling. I used to be that way. My statuses were from the Bible, however, they covered the pain that I was feeling and kept me in the victim mentality. My pain created filters over my eyes when I read the Word of God and once I felt that I had an answer that justified my victim mentality, I posted on Facebook and I would get several likes. It made me feel good, but the likes were only because I gave an answer that also justified *their* victim mentality.

I posted truth relevant to my pain; not THEE Truth.

When you find yourself in a painful situation, it's best that you find a therapist, dedicate time to prayer, and take the time to heal —

especially if you're a preacher. I say this not to "come for" my brothers and sisters in Christ, but to remind them of the call on their life and hold them accountable because people are following you. Because of the cross that you carry and the Truth that you represent, people will automatically look to you for the answer to their problem — whether they say it or not. They're watching.

And like Jesus did on the cross (while hanging in excruciating physical pain and stinging emotional pain), you must still put your pain aside and share the Gospel in love (not your relevant truth) to those who need it most.

When the thief hanging on the cross next to him said, "Save yourself", Jesus could have clapped back; but it wasn't in God's Will to clap back. It was in God's Will to meet the request of the other thief and offer eternal life to him.

But if Jesus would have let His pain speak for Him (including the betrayal that He was experiencing), He could have read those thieves up and down; and technically, He would have been right but, being technically right can lead you right out of God's will. It would also keep onlookers who don't know Christ from seeing the love that's tenderly wrapped up in the Truth.

God will have you endure painful seasons because sometimes it's your pain that will anchor you in Him. Not only that, but it develops and prepares you for your next season. Why? Because before you experience true healing and resurrection, you have to experience pain. You have to sit in it. You can't run out.

I had to learn that. I didn't know how "sick" and broken I was until I had to sit in my pain. If I had done something wrong, I lied. This was due to the fear of rejection from people and wanting to be accepted. This combination was doing the exact thing that I was trying to avoid doing — sabotaging relationships.

I speak about my Spiritual mother a lot and it's because she literally loved the "mess" out of me. She had to make tough decisions to pull the potential that she saw in me, out of me. She was consistent in it. However, I wasn't always consistent in the love that I showed her. I loved her — no doubt — I was ready to fight and defend her at all costs. But because I didn't believe that I was worthy of being loved the way that she had been loving me as a daughter, I would do everything that I could to keep her loving me — which, at times, included not being honest.

The last time I lied to her was when Holy Spirit was doing something new in my life. He was healing me. And although it was comfortable to sit in the lie and be safe, I had no peace. Holy Spirit kept nudging me to call and tell the truth. So, within hours, I got up, called her, and told the truth. It wasn't pretty, but I was free. I was able to exhale and breathe after telling the truth.

But it was still painful. What hurt the most was seeing how I hurt the woman that invested so much in me when she didn't have to. And still — in her pain, she loved me.

Telling the truth wasn't enough. She desired that I be healed. And to do so, I was sat down. No preaching. No leading intercessory prayer. Anything that required me to pour out from my vessel went away for a season. Months. And it was painful.

For the majority of my life, I served in church; so to not serve in any capacity that I desired, hurt me to my core. But I needed to be healed. And I needed to prioritize my healing because my issue was silently killing my purpose. It didn't matter how great I preached, prophesied, or prayed — I needed to be healed so that I could walk in the integrity that was required for my vocation.

I spent nights thinking about relocating to another state, because I couldn't join another church in the same city knowing my heart was still with my church and leader. I wanted to completely uproot from where I was and start new, but that was only a response to my pain and the discomfort that was necessary for my development.

HEAL PREACHER

I wanted to leave but God said, "Stay." So, I stayed, and I submitted to the healing. Standing on the other side of this, not only are my eyes are wide open but now my heart is wide opened. God has placed me in positions where I experienced similar betrayal that my Spiritual mother went through with me; and because I saw the example of Christ through her, I was able to navigate through my betrayal by making the tough decisions to love my betrayers in spite of. I understand the struggle of truly loving and being all in with people who still struggle with love due to the unresolved pain of their past.

But I still love them, because love healed me.

It's difficult to accept tough love from people that you genuinely and authentically love. Most people nowadays would leave the church if they're sat down. If this ever happens to you, then do me a favor. Before you make a decision to leave, I want you to ask yourself what was the reason you were sat down? And reminisce on times spent with your leader — what is their heart toward you?

Most times when you feel excruciating pain, your natural response is to scream and be vocal. You're not able to see the truth about anything because the pain you feel runs deep. My advice: have your moment, but don't make any moves or major decisions from that place. Wait until your vision becomes clearer and you're able to breathe a little easier. And most importantly, seek the Lord and not Facebook.

Being on the other side of healing, I'm able to identify hurting people a lot clearer through their behaviors and mental processes. Daily, I was seeing how broken preachers were, but they were still trying to preach (on Facebook) in the midst of their pain. Their Facebook post was the vocal response to the excruciating pain they were feeling. I remained quiet for months, then with Holy Spirit's approval, I addressed it.

Here is what I posted…

"#preacher
Be healed. Prioritize your healing.

HEAL PREACHER

I never post concerning the body of Christ because I absolutely dislike the division that I see where Christians are attacking, challenging (or whatever you want to call it) other Christians... our fellow brothers and sisters.

But I also hurt at the sight of seeing many preachers bleeding on other people. I used to be guilty of it — so I know. I'm VERY familiar with it.

This gospel that we carry will lead to some people potentially hurting us...

If I can offer some wisdom/advice, instead of denying the hurt/pain, deal with it. Dealing with it is the only way that you will maintain a pure heart so that you can love others authentically, and continue to rightly divide the Word of Truth.

Unresolved pain becomes a filter and begins to pervert the original nature of things that we see and/or try to comprehend. In other words, it's an open door for the enemy to slither in and deceive you. And you will begin to preach from pain rather than preaching with power.

Don't go to Facebook or any other social media platform to voice pain. The validation from others feels good but the validation from God feels so much better. There is healing in His presence. And get this — healing is an ongoing journey. You may not be healed overnight. So choose to keep pursuing God until He purifies you and you're able to genuinely and authentically love those who caused you pain.

Also, there is relief in venting. But instead of the internet, go to trusted individuals who can be strength to you in your time of weakness.

It's okay to be broken... just don't break everybody else. Be healed. God wants you healed because there is soooo much work to do.

Don't get so lost in culture that you lose sight of Christ and what He desires for you.

HEAL PREACHER

People want deliverance not drama."

To preach powerfully, healing is required. Don't delay the process by ignoring the intensity of your pain or ignoring the guidance or voice of a trusted individual. If you need to sit down, then sit down and be healed.

Take it from me. You'll be better from it. I love being on this side of freedom and I don't have a desire to look back to the bondage I was once in.

My relationships (in all aspects) are better, including my relationship with my Spiritual mother. It could just be me, but I believe that we're closer than we've ever been since I've known her... that's my girl (respectfully lol).

Preacher, God wants healing for you. You have not seen the power of God in your preaching until you have submitted completely to God's healing. Let Him heal you. Lives are depending on your healing, including your family. If you have someone who loves you enough to prioritize your healing when you're not, heed to that advice.

It's time for the TRUE YOU to arise. Your family is waiting on it. Your coworkers are waiting on it. Your neighbors are waiting on it.

Choose to commit to the discomfort just for a little while, because your healing is worth it girl!

HEAL PREACHER

CHAPTER 13

I Stopped Breathing

Did you know that it was possible for you to not breathe and still live?

I began going to a chiropractor who was also a nutritionist. After a few adjustments, he gave me a script to have my blood taken at a local lab. Once he received the results, he called me back in.

He reviewed the blood work with me line by line. Then he got to the carbon dioxide (CO_2) levels. He stated, "Now look at this. This is on the low side. Do you know what that tells me?"

Not knowing exactly what CO_2 indicated, I answered, "No…"

He said, "You're not breathing."

I STOPPED BREATHING

I was completely blown away that a simple blood test could give a man that knew very little about me, insight of how I was living.

When he said it, it clicked immediately. I reflected back on one of my first meetings with my Spiritual mom and pastor. We were at her home in her family room, eating Publix subs. I was sitting across from her on one of her sofas. She looked at me. I looked back. Then she said, "Why are you uptight? Loosen up. Breathe. You're safe."

I didn't know how to loosen up, mainly because I thought I was already loose. I smiled easily, told jokes, and laughed but still wasn't breathing. At the time, I was afraid of messing up or saying the wrong thing that would end up ruining another relationship.

But God eventually healed me from that fear. However, because I lived like that for years, the effect that it had on my body was still there and I didn't even realize it — I wasn't breathing. I was still holding my breath.

Trauma from my past trained my body how to hold my breath and still live. However, what I didn't know was that it was affecting how my body operated internally. My blood couldn't carry the necessary oxygen to the different organs of my body because I wasn't breathing.

The doctor continued, "I want you to practice these breathing exercises to train your body to breathe again."

There's a saying that says, "Life will take your breath away." I knew it to be true, but I thought that it was only for a moment. However, when you've experienced rejection after rejection, tragedy after tragedy, and huge life changes that won't let up, sometimes you don't notice that your breath never returned (that is, until your body starts talking back).

You cannot stop life from happening, but as life happens, don't forget to breathe. God wants you to keep breathing. Adopting techniques to survive through trauma is sometimes necessary, but it should also be temporary. God is a Restorer and when He restores, He restores you and everything connected to you — if you allow Him.

"Trust in the Lord with all your heart, and do not rely on your own understanding; in all your ways know him, and he will make your paths straight." (Proverbs 3:5-6 CSB)

When you rely on your own understanding, you rob yourself from God's best. You are not going to know all of the details, but you are safe with giving God all of your heart. He knows the details. Sometimes He doesn't tell you the details so that you can continue to breathe in the process.

Breathing symbolizes awareness. To thrive in life, you must be aware. Holding your breath limits your awareness and shifts your focus from resting to waiting on a threat.

It's time for you to rest in God's arms. Relax. And breathe.

If you're not breathing, you're not living. God wants you to live.

Choose today to give Him all of your heart and just breathe. You're in safe hands. Trusting God will release the stress, anxiety, and trauma that is causing you to hold your breath. Trusting God releases your breath.

Let go and breathe girl!

I STOPPED BREATHING

CHAPTER 14

FOMO

I was getting to know a young man and was hoping that our relationship would progress into what we both desired — marriage.

I really liked him. He was handsome, intelligent, a family man, honest, hardworking, and he loved Jesus. Each day we talked, it seemed like being together was exactly what God desired for us. I began to see the light at the end of the tunnel where my season of singleness was coming to an end.

So I thought…

After nearly 2 months of trying to get to know each other, I noticed that his focus shifted. I very rarely received good night and good morning messages. We stopped talking every day. It seemed his interest began to fade, and I was clueless as to why.

Naturally, I thought this was the doing of the devil — trying to separate us to stop what God was doing in us. So, I began to fight the best way that I knew how. I began sending good morning and good night messages. And I attempted to initiate conversations throughout the day. I did what I thought was necessary to keep our connection as lively as it once was.

Sometimes he answered and sometimes he didn't. And when he answered it was short and to the point. After a week or so of trying to preserve what we started, I finally had a conversation with him to find out what was going on.

He mentioned that he was still interested and knows what God showed him regarding us, but he was preoccupied with life. I respected his honesty and told him that I was here whenever he was ready.

Sounds crazy, right? Who in their right mind would entertain just an idea of a relationship? (Not a relationship… just an idea.) Not married, but hanging around until *"mister"* got himself ready to be with you?

Sis was guilty of this… I am Sis.

I was guilty and the root of me doing this was desperation. I was at a point where I desired companionship, a partner in ministry, and more kids (just to name a few things), and this guy appearing out of nowhere seemed like an answer to my prayers. So, I didn't want to let go and miss out on what he and I could be. I had a huge case of FOMO — Fear of Missing Out.

But sometimes letting go could be the biggest blessing you may ever experience.

I kept contacting him and I kept getting short answers. Then, one day he contacted me — I was ecstatic! We talked for all of 5 minutes, and then he left me hanging.

I said to myself, *"I'll wait for him to contact me later today."* He never did. So right before I went to sleep, I was about to contact him and Holy Spirit said, *"No."*

FOMO

I put my phone down. Then, FOMO came back, and I picked it up again and Holy Spirit politely repeated His instructions, *"No."*

I put my phone down, turned over and went to sleep. I had made up in my mind that if he didn't contact me by the time I woke up, I would send a "check-in" text.

The next morning came. I read my Bible, then checked my phone — nothing. I proceeded to text him, and Holy Spirit stopped me and said *"No"* again.

But I didn't want to let go of what seemed to be good.

Then I realized what was happening…

Holy Spirit telling me no repeatedly was keeping me from picking up the cycle that was rooted in insecurity again. His *"No"* was my protection.

Instead of allowing God to do His thing, I felt like I had to control it because it was going a different way than what I was expecting. I felt the need to take action because I refused to let go of what seemed to be a *"God thing"*. But here's the key to "God things" …

If it *is*, in fact, a *"God thing"*, then you have to allow God to do His thing. Simply put, you have to trust Him. It's okay to let go.

Holy Spirit telling me *no* gave me strength. It reminded me of my value and purpose — which is probably what the young man needed to see. He needed to see that I not only knew my worth and value, but I also stood strongly in it. Boys want to be chased. Real men love to chase. It's in their DNA. It's a part of their purpose, but you have to be and know that you are worth the chase.

It is not my responsibility to chase a man or try to make him try to like me out of fear of missing out on something that never was. Furthermore, that last *"No"* from Holy Spirit reminded me that I could be doing better things with my time rather than doing things that will take me out of my purpose.

FOMO

Having FOMO is the quickest way for you to easily walk out of your purpose. The root is fear. Fear will cause you to lose focus which in turn causes you to drift further and further away from your identity, value and power. It breeds insecurity which blinds you from seeing the blessing in your situation *"as is"*, because you're trying to control what could be.

Be healed from fear and rest in the assurance that your now doesn't determine or alter God's best for you. Fear will cause you to hold on to things that hold no value in your life.

But the wisest man in the world once said…

"Trust in the Lord with all your heart, and do not rely on your own understanding; in all your ways know him, and he will make your paths straight. Don't be wise in your own eyes; fear the Lord and turn away from evil." Proverbs 3:5–7 CSB

When you hold on to what seems to make more sense to you, then the very thing that you fear of missing out on becomes your god. Releasing your understanding and choosing to trust God releases God's best for you — unhindered.

When Holy Spirit says *"No,"* it's for your good. It's an awakening call so that your destiny and blessings are preserved. *"No"* will also escort you into the freedom that you've been praying for. It will realign you into God's timing.

Adhere to Holy Spirit's *"No"*. It's for your good and progression.

If you fear anything, then fear God. It brings you in alignment with His timing.

When you are realigned to God's timing, the only things that you are missing out on are heartache and destruction. God's timing may be a hard pill for you to swallow right now because you don't have all of the details, but His provision always leads to His promise. It's the safest place that you can be.

You're safe in God's timing. There is no reason to fear.

Let go of what's hindering you from God's best and HEAL Girl!

HEAL GIRL

CHAPTER 15

Let it Go

I was at a hotel where a conference was going on. I entered the lobby area where the vendors were. There were several people selling purses. It seemed like they wanted to make sure that we had an easy way to carry our belongings.

I entered the room where the conference was being held and shortly after, we went into prayer. I saw someone who I knew was an amazing intercessor. She was holding an adorable baby. We prayed together and shortly after I began talking with this intercessor, the baby suddenly lunged towards me to give me a gummy kiss. As the baby lunged, the intercessor shouted, "NOOO!" And we fell through the crack of the floor to a lower level.

We anxiously were looking for our way back to the higher level. The intercessor held on to the baby as we raced to find an elevator. A man saw us and realized that we belonged on a higher level, so he showed us to the elevator.

The intercessor with the baby got on with ease. I entered the elevator but was pulled back by a force. Something was grabbing the fanny pack that I was wearing and wouldn't let me get on the elevator unless I let the fanny pack go.

The elevator door was closing so I used all my strength to hold on to what I was carrying, and was able to enter the elevator before the door closed.

We arrived at the right level and the guy who was leading us told us where to go to get back to where we were — the conference. I heard him talking but missed the instructions because I was trying to make sure that I had everything with me. Then I saw the intercessor running with the baby. Surprised to see her running, I looked at the man and he said, "Go! Follow her!"

LET IT GO

So, I ran but I was behind. She was navigating through the crowd of people and very focused on where she was going. I was getting slowed down by the people and became afraid that I would lose her.

She turned a corner. I turned the corner. And then it happened…

A large group of people came in between me and my vision of her. I got through the people but had no idea where she went. I was lost. And didn't know where to go.

I eventually got to where I needed to be however, it took me much longer because, although small, I wouldn't let go of my bag.

Your next level, your ability to thrive could very well be stunted because you are holding on to things that no longer have significance in your life. In order to move forward into your next, you have to be willing to let go of all things that no longer have purpose in your life.

An easy way to tell when something no longer has purpose in your life, is realizing that you're able to thrive without it. It may be uncomfortable to be without it, but it's only uncomfortable because having it has become familiar to you. Familiarity breeds comfort.

The healing that you've been praying for is accessible. You can break the never-ending cycle in your life. But you must be willing to let go of the bag. Let go of what you've carried.

In 1 Kings chapter nineteen, Elijah met Elisha. Elijah left one place and found Elisha while he walking to his next assignment. The Bible says that when Elijah walked by Elisha, he threw his mantle on Him. Elisha ran after Elijah and ended up burning all he had to follow Elijah.

What has been thrown on you? And are you aware enough to realize that what has been thrown on you is worthy enough for you to leave all else behind?

LET IT GO

Healing births awareness. And awareness opens the door to your new level.

HEAL Girl! because your new level is waiting.

HEAL GIRL

CHAPTER 16

Healing Equals Legacy

Friend: "How's your son?"

Me: "Growing too fast. Becoming a young man. It's a new level of parenting. 'Letting go.'"

When my son was in elementary school, people would always tell me, "Embrace this time because it goes fast." I would listen, but I had no idea how fast it would go.

My son is now in high school, and I often find myself looking at old pictures of him — baby photos, kindergarten pics — and I reflect on the journey and joys of parenting. Then, reality kicks in and I realize that I'm now getting him ready for adulthood; and I begin to wonder, "How did I get here so soon?"

Being a single mother to a boy, I didn't have all of the answers. There were specific incidents that happened where not even my family had the answers. I had to figure it out and determine what would be best for my son.

The best and only way that I knew to do that was to seek God. Through seeking Him, He cancelled a negative diagnosis that was given to my son, He healed my son supernaturally from a heart defect, and He carried my son through emotional heartbreak (just to name a few things).

As I sought the LORD on how to raise my son, God was raising me. Every stage that I went through with God, modeled how I was to raise my son. He loved me, gave me grace, was patient with me, and let me go when He saw that I was capable of making decisions that honored Him.

In this parenting journey, letting go and giving my son independence has been one of the hardest (yet most rewarding) things that I have done. It's the hardest because sometimes I have to watch him fall. However, it's rewarding when I see that he was able to learn from that fall.

When you're a parent, it's your desire to catch and protect your child from every fall (and until they reach a certain age, it's completely necessary). However, if you continue to be their cushion to fall back on, they will become stagnant in their development mentally and emotionally, and you, as the parent, will become worn out as a result.

Falling is necessary and it is normal. No one wants to see their child in pain from a fall, but pain is a teacher. So now instead of catching my son from every fall, I'm helping him navigate through the pain and confusion experienced after the fall, which teaches him how to recover.

We can't escape the battles that we have in life. But the assurance that we have is that God knows about every battle, and He sees us in the battle. Sometimes He will be silent, but that doesn't mean that He isn't present.

HEAL GIRL

One of the greatest joys that parents have is to watch their children take all of the lessons they've learned and thrive in life. That's LEGACY.

Sometimes God will be silent in some of the most painful and challenging moments in your life, but His eye has never left you. He's watching you with confidence because He knows that He has equipped you for the decision or challenge before you.

A parent letting go is an outward acknowledgment of a child maturing. It's a part of growth.

As you let go of things that have held you in bondage mentally, physically, emotionally, and spiritually, it not only displays healing, but it displays maturity.

When you let go, God lets go and releases more to you.

When you let go, you make way for God to give you more.

HEALING EQUALS LEGACY

He's able to trust you with more because He has seen you go through your process of healing, and you have been proven trustworthy to handle more without constant supervision.

You've prayed to be trusted with more and that comes through you being healed. God is not going to release what you cannot handle.

"Therefore, if anyone is in Christ, he is a new creation; the old has passed away, and see, the new has come!" 2 Corinthians 5:17 CSB

A lot of people have accepted Christ, but they have failed to allow what's old to pass away. They are not able to focus and thrive as a new creation because the wounds from the past still bring pain. It distracts them from fully accepting the new that is available to them.

It's hard to let go of the old when you're still staring and picking at the wound. When wounds heal, it's ugly and rough. It sticks out from the rest of your body which is why you are tempted to pick at it — because you don't want to look at it.

But in order to experience healing, you must be willing to face the ugliness of your past. The longer it goes untreated, the longer you will remain in a broken cycle.

When you accept Christ, you accept a new DNA. You're a new creature. However, to experience that newness in its fullness, you must let go of what's been. Letting go is a part of your new DNA because it's the key to healing.

And healing = legacy.

God gave His only Son to be crucified so that you can be healed. He wants you to be healed because He wants to see you thrive in life.

Choose today to accept your Godly DNA by letting go of what's been and walking into what God has promised you — HEAL Girl!

You have the right to let go.

HEALING EQUALS LEGACY

CONCLUSION

The Bottom Line

Heal
/hēl/
verb
: to become sound and healthy again.
(Similar: make better, make well, cure, treat successfully, restore to health)

Let go. Trust God. Be whole. Be healed.

THE BOTTOM LINE

BONUS CHAPTER

War for Your Healing

Healing is a beautiful thing and it's my prayer that *HEAL Girl!* has brought you closer to living healed.

As you begin to walk in your healing, don't be ignorant of Satan's devices; meaning, just because you're healed doesn't mean that all of your obstacles disappear. You *will* experience adversity that sometimes happen almost immediately after your healing manifests.

It's necessary that you war (or fight) for your healing in the process, but don't neglect warring to maintain your healing.

Unfortunately, many end up backtracking in their healing process because after they begin to feel relief and see progress, they let their guard down. This is the moment that the enemy slides in and begins to influence a situation to bring you back to a familiar place.

Choose today to resist him.

In Ephesians chapter 6, Paul gave practical instruction on how to be successful and thrive in life. He tells children to obey their parents so that they may live long. He tells fathers to not provoke their children but to instruct them in the Lord (this is legacy!).

Paul continued by telling us to obey those over us as unto the Lord. He tells us not to fake it but instead to put our all into what we do. He tells us to have a good attitude as unto the Lord because as we serve, God will reward us.

Then, he says to be strengthened in the Lord and put on the full armor of God. God desires that we are not only healed, but that we thrive in our healing. We are called to walk in authority in the domain that God has trusted us with. In order to do so, you must choose to gird up on a daily basis.

HEAL GIRL

Your success is in how you fight. Reading this may seem intimidating and overwhelming, but God will give you the strength to stand in the midst of temptation, uncertainty, and pain.

Maintaining your healing is just as important as receiving your healing. The enemy's goal is to distract you to get you off track. He is relentless, but you have power over him.

Put on the full armor of God. Don't shrink when you begin to experience obstacles. Ask God for direction and guidance as you go through the obstacle, and stand firm.

Not all battles are not meant for you to flee. Some are meant for you to stand so that you can be revealed to others in your healed identity.

When Jesus healed people by telling them to take up their bed and walk, I'm sure that these people who were once bedridden received many looks of confusion and judgement. Everyone wasn't used to seeing them healed. They were used to seeing them sick and immobile.

WAR FOR YOUR HEALING

Your healing enables you. It mobilizes you; and as much as you'd like to believe that everyone would readily accept you in your new state, that's not always the case.

Just because you're healed doesn't mean that others see you as healed. Some people will only see you in a sick place because that's what they are used to. However, you don't have to respond to their vision. Choose to walk in God's vision.

Maintain your healing. Stand in it. Walk in it. Don't let your past carry you – God has given you the power to carry it.

Gone are the days that you shrink or bow to the familiar or what has been. You are a new creation.

Walk in the image and power of God.

Adversity will come. Expect it. But always choose to war for your healing.

As you war for your healing, choose to make these declarations over your life:

- I declare that strongholds are demolished and will not return. Thank You Lord for giving me the discernment to quickly identify the works of the enemy and to stand strong in the midst of adversity.

- I declare that my body is strong and my mind is strong.

- I demolish every argument and pretension that sets itself up against the knowledge of God, and I take captive every thought and make it obedient to Christ according to 2 Corinthians10:4-5

- I speak to fear and by the power of Holy Spirit and the Blood of Jesus, I command the spirit of fear to leave me now. I declare that God didn't give me the spirit of fear but of power, love, and a sound mind, according to 2 Timothy 1:7.

- I embrace Your perfect love that drives out all fear. I thrive in Your love, and I am free from fear.

- You have delivered me from sin and healed me. I am made whole in You.

- Every enemy that rises up against me will be defeated. Though the enemy comes in one way, he will flee seven different ways, according to Deuteronomy 28:7.

- No matter what is going on in my life, I declare that I am more than a conqueror through You, Father, because you love me, according to Romans 8:37-39

- Thank You for loving and healing me. In Jesus' Name, Amen.

NOTES

NOTES

NOTES

NOTES

NOTES

NOTES

NOTES

NOTES

NOTES

NOTES

What Did You Think of "HEAL Girl!"?

Thank you for purchasing **"HEAL Girl!"**. You could have picked any number of books to read, but you chose this book and for that I am extremely grateful.

It is my prayer that **"HEAL Girl!"** has added value and quality to your daily life. If so, then it would be really nice if you could do *at least* one of the following:

1. Post a review on Amazon.com
2. Share this book with your friends and family
3. Share this book on Facebook, Instagram, Threads, X (*formerly Twitter*), and/or TikTok with the hashtag #HEALgirl

If you have enjoyed **"HEAL Girl!"** and found value in reading it, I'd love to hear from you and hope that you could take some time to post a review and share it with others.

As always, my prayers are with you and your loved ones. May you be enriched with God's blessings forevermore.

ABOUT THE AUTHOR

Tiffany White is an accomplished author, writing coach, and dedicated servant of her community and faith. Known for her inspiring words and unwavering commitment to helping others, Tiffany's life is a testament to resilience, faith, and the power of purpose.

With five published books to her name, Tiffany has carved a niche for herself in the world of literature. Her books, each a unique journey of self-discovery and empowerment, have touched the hearts of countless readers. Beyond her own literary pursuits, Tiffany serves as a writing coach, guiding aspiring authors on the path to bringing their own stories to life in just 30 days.

Tiffany's commitment to excellence is evident in her academic achievements. She graduated summa cum laude with a Bachelor's degree in Business Administration from American Intercontinental University. Her strong educational foundation and entrepreneurial spirit paved the way for a successful career in marketing and as a business owner.

Tiffany's devotion to her faith is at the core of her identity. She proudly serves as an associate Pastor at Oasis Church International under the leadership of Pastor Cassandra V. Fulwood. Her faith is not confined to the pulpit; she is a Christian influencer who uses her platform to inspire and uplift others, sharing the message of Jesus, hope, faith, and love.

Tiffany's reach extends beyond the written word. She hosts the SOLID Saturdays: Prayer + Inspiration Podcast, a source of spiritual nourishment that brightens Saturday mornings for many internationally. But her greatest joy is being a mother to her teenage son and cultivating his gifts. He is the center of her world.

Above all, Tiffany's deepest desire is to please God in every aspect of her life. She lives by the principles of faith, love, integrity, and service, embodying the grace and strength that come from a life rooted in God.

Tiffany White's journey is one of empowerment, inspiration, and faith. Her books, coaching, ministry, and podcasting reflect her unwavering commitment to making a positive impact on the lives of others. Through her words and actions, she continues to uplift, inspire, and lead by example, showing that a life lived in service to others is a life truly well-lived.

Connect with Tiffany on her journey as she continues to inspire and empower through her books, coaching, ministry, and podcast.

Website: www.simplytiffany.net

Instagram: @iamsimplytiffany

Facebook:
https://www.facebook.com/TiffiBee/

TikTok: @imsimplytiffany

www.ingramcontent.com/pod-product-compliance
Lightning Source LLC
Chambersburg PA
CBHW070742060526
44119CB00070B/72